MW01194557

S.A.L.S.A.: Finding Your Rhythm to Success

ISBN 1453825193

Edited by Ashley Werner, solutionssubmitted@gmail.com

Book cover by Sarah Dupree, www.sarahdzines.com

Introduction and Dedication

Welcome to this unique tool and experience. What you've picked up won't just touch your mind, but your body and your soul as well.

As you move through this book's pages, you will work through three different levels.

The first of these will open you up to the concept of S.A.L.S.A. and its five key elements (and we're talking about the dance, not the food, although their origins are much the same). This will give you a great foundation for the rest of the program.

The second level will be about connections; it's quite possible that after you've finished this section, you'll find yourself connecting with people you've never seen and may never know. You won't be connected physically, of course—but by S.A.L.S.A. and what it means. There aren't ever any trap doors or hidden messages in what it says: it's just about relating to other people. As you read the stories and experiences from other people, I'm sure that you'll begin to understand what they felt. You can then relate this to your own feelings. It's crucial to remember, after all, that in both good times and bad, we're never alone. There's always something positive in our lives that can keep us going.

The last section is designed to keep you thinking. There are twenty-six letters in our English alphabet, so I've put up a key word for each letter. Some letters even have multiple words attached to them to keep us pushing, praying, preparing, positioning, and performing.

(Did I miss any P's? Ha ha.) These are the words to write onto note cards that you can go back to whenever you want—whenever you want to be reminded of who you are and what you're capable of, right from A to Z. I think you'll enjoy them, and you'll also be free to add your own along the way—so please do. The section is called "The ABCs in Your Rhythm to Success." Have fun with it, and don't forget to add your own rhythm along the way.

A True Lead—Preface

Salsa has had a huge impact on our lives. For us, what began as a hobby has become a shared passion, profession, and way of life. When the two of us met while attending Georgia State University, neither of us could have ever predicted that we would one day have our own dance company—or that we would be performing and teaching all over the country!

When we decided that we would be partners, Niya had never danced Salsa before (although she was a classically trained dancer), and I was only at the beginner level. However, we both loved to dance and thought that it would be both beneficial and convenient to grow as dancers together; we were already spending a substantial amount of time together studying. In the midst of mid-terms, finals, research papers, etc., Salsa dancing provided us with an excellent outlet to relieve the overwhelming stress that is common among college students with heavy workloads. We learned how to balance work and play, and we gained many friends of various races and backgrounds who share our passion.

We now help new dancers who are seeking guidance and even teach Salsa at GSU so that current students can take advantage of the same opportunities we had while they are on campus. The satisfaction we get from spreading the art is immense. From our transition from college social dancers to student performers to company directors, our love for the dance and our bonds with the community have steadily grown. Salsa has brought us enlightenment, joy, and an overall sense of accomplishment and well-being. Who knows what it could bring you...

Hope to see you on the dance floor!

Allen Germaine & Niya Patel, Atlanta, GA
Co-Directors of Proyecto Barrio Dance
Company
"Unifying Cultures Through Dance"

This book is more than your everyday read: it's a small tool that you can use to develop your mind, body, and soul. S.A.L.S.A. is not an intense piece of literature that will boggle your brain, but it is a work that will give you a little relief from the craziness that may consume your life from time to time.

Throughout the pages, you will have the opportunity to share your thoughts, as the book relates to what's covered in the workshop. Express whatever you want as you see fit. If you have experienced the workshop in the past, this is something to take with you as a reminder of the time we spent together, the fun we had, and the things you have learned. If you have yet to experience the workshop, I must tell you that our encounter will be a great one wherever you are in your thoughts and drive. Please give yourself and me a chance.

We are born to be great and are already far better than we think. However you use S.A.L.S.A., it can only strengthen your skill set and abilities as you move through life with all of its situations and obstacles. The program is also more fun than you can begin to imagine, especially when you understand and value the principles that will be introduced.

I must tell you now that I love Salsa dancing. I love Salsa dancing like peanut butter loves jelly. I love Salsa like you might love your mom's home cooking. I don't live where my parents are, so I must also tell you that, at times, Salsa is my home away from home. It doesn't provide the same things that home does, but it can bring me to a similar place. Sometimes activities or experiences aren't exactly the same in our lives, but they can still bring us to familiar places in our thoughts and in our hearts.

When I dance Salsa, so many things happen to me. I feel free. I feel happy. I feel at home because the dance has helped me grow, learn, and appreciate something that is different. It has also given me different perspectives on life and the people who live life as I do as well as those who live it differently. Everyone dances for different reasons, but I really hope that we all get a positive result from it. This is why the S.A.L.S.A. workshop has been developed and also why it has quickly become one of the most requested programs throughout the country on college campuses. It has also been a useful tool for businesses that want to realize staff development and enrichment.

In general, Salsa dancing has become even more popular throughout the world as the years have passed. If you checked out some simple history about Salsa, you would soon find out that Cuba has been given credit for its beginning around a century ago. Many countries of Latin American descent have since added their own flavors, styles, and feelings to make it what it is today. As I understand things, New York actually came up with the term "Salsa"—mainly to describe all of the different countries that initially influenced this dance that we enjoy so much.

Salsa takes us to a combination of places in our minds and hearts. When you listen to Salsa and even other Latin music, you will hear drums, instruments, and many more sounds. Lots of those drums and rhythms originally came from Africa. Rhythm is dear to everyone who walks the earth, and those rhythms from Africa allowed people to communicate through song and beats. We use those same rhythms to communicate today. Later, as Africans and Europeans mixed in the islands and namely Cuba, the rest began to evolve in music and in song.

I suppose I could go deeper, but I feel like that's a good start, isn't it? Who would have thought that history could be so interesting?

Finally, as always, I'd like to thank those people who made a way before me, which allows me to enjoy this part of my life today.

S.A.L.S.A. is an acronym that stands for five key principles. Each one is related to dancing as well as life, and they are all intended to help you out on your journey through the world. They may not always come in sequence, but they will always come—and when they do, knowing how to handle them will let you move to your own healthy, productive, and satisfying rhythm.

The words that live within Salsa are Support, Act, Learn, Strive, and Accept. So...here we go!

Support

Support (n.): *a person or thing that gives aid or assistance; something that serves as a foundation, prop, or brace*[1]

In terms of the Salsa dance, support translates into standing firm, staying balanced, and keeping a straight posture as you prepare to move. It's all about mastering the basics: if you have a strong foundation, you'll be able to build on it and dance more successfully in the future. You'll continue to improve because of how well you're supported.

The same applies to you as a person: having strong support is vital to achieving whatever you want to in your life. As we go further and achieve more, we need more sup-

---

[1] http://www.dictionary.com.

port—the things that got us through yesterday won't necessarily get us through tomorrow. This means that we always need to be on the lookout for ways to prop ourselves up. To put it in perspective, the amount of support we have can be in direct correlation to who we are as people and what we're capable of achieving.

Try imagining two buildings to make the situation clearer: one is a one-story house, and the other is a skyscraper. While both are structures, they don't need the same amount of support to stay standing. As you continue on your journey through the world, take the time to build a strong environment around yourself. Decide whether you want to be a house or a skyscraper, and always ensure that your support system has the solid foundation it needs to

match.

Reflections

_____

_____

_____

_____

_____

_____

_____

_____

_____

_____

_____

_____

_____

_____

_____

_____

_____

_____

_____

Reflections

_____

_____

_____

_____

_____

_____

_____

_____

_____

_____

_____

_____

_____

_____

_____

_____

_____

Reflections

_____

_____

_____

_____

_____

_____

_____

_____

_____

_____

_____

_____

_____

_____

_____

_____

_____

_____

_____

_____

Act

Act (n.): *anything done, being done, or to be done; a formal decision; philosophically a state of realization, as opposed to a potentiality*[2] (That last one is deep!)

Acting can be very scary because it always involves risk on some level. In dancing, it's about taking a step and seeing what happens. Most of us will sit on the sidelines saying, "Wow, that looks awesome and like so much fun!" but will never do anything to get involved. Others will get a bit further and start to do something but won't take it seriously out of fear for how they look or what others will say. To be a successful Salsa dancer, you have to be committed to what you're doing—and when

---

[2] http://www.dictionary.com.

you're in a routine, you have to approach each step with absolute certainty.

In life, we have opportunities to act during every experience. Some of you might be in school or in organizations, so you'll even have your support system in place, but you still won't give yourself a real chance or take yourself seriously. Why? Why are you afraid to act? Is it because you don't believe you've got what it takes? Are you afraid that someone will say something about you and your effort? I'll be completely honest with you: everyone has their opinions no matter what. Since they'll talk regardless, why not commit to what you're doing and truly make your effort to act a real one? You're absolutely worth the effort. So long as you have the right **support** in place, your **act** won't be done in vain. Step out onto the dance

floor of life and get busy!

Reflections

Reflections

_____

_____

_____

_____

_____

_____

_____

_____

_____

_____

_____

_____

_____

_____

_____

_____

_____

Reflections

_____

_____

_____

_____

_____

_____

_____

_____

_____

_____

_____

_____

_____

_____

_____

_____

_____

_____

_____

<u>Learn</u>

Learn (v.): *to acquire knowledge or skill by study; to become informed; to memorize*[3]

As we go through life, learning is continuous; I firmly believe that if you aren't learning, you aren't living. Another way of thinking about this is with the Peak to Peak Philosophy. This gets you to imagine that you're at the top of a mountain (the peak) from where you can see the next mountain's peak in the distance. You can then move on to that peak, always trying to get higher than you were before. Learning is the same: you should always be looking out for ways to learn and to improve yourself. If you do this, you'll go far.

---

[3] http://www.dictionary.com.

To link learning with Salsa, I often relate it to golf. If any of you reading this play golf, you might be thinking "no way," but give me a moment to explain. Golf is a game that, for all intents and purposes, can never be completely mastered. Every day you step out onto the course, you have a new perspective and a new goal. No matter how much you know, you can always learn something new, as everyone has a different style that might work for you. This is how Salsa is the same. There are many differ-ent styles in terms of the way people dance the dance and feel the music. All we have to do is learn what works for us and make the absolute best of it.

There are many Salsa dancers and in-structors out there who are continuously learning regardless of how much they seem to know. They all realize that they can get better and are willing to learn so as to do just that. This is something that I particularly love about Salsa dancing: you end up learning even when you don't recognize it. Your mind and body are always working constantly.

Life provides the same opportunities and perspectives. We can always learn from one another and from our teachers in life (who can come in the form of parents, guardians, friends, and even complete strangers). We just have to be willing to learn from them and the situations we find ourselves in. We are all con-tinuously learning, connecting, and communi-cating. Seize the opportunity and learn every day. When you have the proper **support** and are ready to **act**, you'll even be able to **learn** more easily.

Reflections

_____

_____

_____

_____

_____

_____

_____

_____

_____

_____

_____

_____

_____

_____

_____

_____

_____

_____

Reflections

_____

_____

_____

_____

_____

_____

_____

_____

_____

_____

_____

_____

_____

_____

_____

_____

_____

_____

Reflections

_____

_____

_____

_____

_____

_____

_____

_____

_____

_____

_____

_____

_____

_____

_____

_____

_____

_____

_____

Strive

Strive (v.): *to exert one's self vigorously; to make strenuous efforts toward any goal; to contend in opposition, battle, or any conflict; to struggle vigorously or resist; to rival*[4]

As you can see, the dictionary has quite a few definitions for this word, all of which are really motivational. I particularly enjoyed reading the last two when I was putting this book together: when I read "to rival," for example, I thought of the best sports rivals and the best competitions you can ever imagine. I then thought about how we all have rivals: it's always You vs. Mediocrity, Good vs. Great, Ordinary vs. Extraordinary, Struggle vs. Progress, etc. As the definition also suggests, striving

---

[4] http://www.dictionary.com.

might involve some struggle, effort, and even sweat and tears. You'll love it when you decide to live it, though, I promise! Ha ha! Feel the rhythm, hear the music of life, and start striving to play your tune.

Striving seems to be a major hiccup in many of our lives. Why? Because we're part of a culture that thinks it knows it all. Once we've applied, learned, and acknowledged the first three principles of S.A.L.S.A., this sometimes means that we take the striving for granted. We might think, "Well...I already know how to do what this program's teaching, so what will I get out of focusing on striving for it?" This leads to us not stretching ourselves any further than what's average. When you decide to strive and commit yourself to being better and doing better, however, you can turn your life around.

It's not always easy: you might start feeling that too much is coming at you at once, and this might lead you to question your choice to strive. Don't do that. When you experience hardship, difficulty, and stress as a result of striving, take it as a sign that you're moving in the direction. After all, when you make a conscious decision to strive, you also take responsibility for where you want to end up.

If striving were at the end of an equation, it would look like this: **Support** + **Action** + **Learning** = **Striving**. When we think of **support**, we think of foundations. Without proper foundations, our **actions** will be in vain and will not sustain themselves. Once we have sought out, gained, and recognized positive **support**, we are able to **act** appropriately, and through those **actions**, we **learn** what works and what doesn't. When you know what works, you **strive**! I hope this makes sense to you: every-thing should have its order so we don't put the cart before the horse and so we don't try to push a string. We don't get anywhere when we execute those types of things. You are better than you think you are. Yes, **YOU!**

Reflections

_____

_____

_____

_____

_____

_____

_____

_____

_____

_____

_____

_____

_____

_____

_____

_____

_____

_____

Reflections

_____

_____

_____

_____

_____

_____

_____

_____

_____

_____

_____

_____

_____

_____

_____

_____

_____

_____

Reflections

_____

_____

_____

_____

_____

_____

_____

_____

_____

_____

_____

_____

_____

_____

_____

_____

_____

_____

Accept

Accept (v.): *undertake responsibility, duties, or honors; to understand*[5]

When you accept the responsibility for something that has happened, it doesn't mean that it was your fault. It simply means that you've accepted the situation for what it is, and that it will not dictate how you continue to function as a result.

In schools, on college campuses, and in businesses and offices across the country, bad things are happening. I don't like to think of these moments, but am reminded of Virginia Tech, Northern Illinois, or even the University of Texas at Austin in the 1960s. These are extremes in terms of people shifting their though-

---

[5] http://www.dictionary.com.

ts, feelings, or existence to a point of no return, but they are still realities. The Discovery Channel hostage situation and quite possibly even homeless people are other examples of lack of acceptance. Why, do you ask? Those incidents involve people who have been through something. They have had an experience that has moved them in such a way and they were not able to RECOVER. If you've heard me speak before, then you know that word very well and how it applies.

In terms of acceptance, I will use someone who is homeless as an example. I am not homeless, though I have talked to some homeless people, and we have all seen them around at some point or another. I don't think that homeless people are bad people. I don't feel like they are evil. However, I do assume that they might have had a series of issues and obstacles in their lives that they have failed to accept in the proper capacity. Maybe they were not able to undertake the responsibility of whatever they were going through and, as a result, lost their job. This lost job perhaps then turned into a lost car, and this lost car then turned into a lost house. Sometimes things just keep on going and going and adding up and pushing us. When this happens, I challenge you to stay the course.

Accept some of life's situations and issues and move forward, because S.A.L.S.A. is cyclical. Once you accept, you go right back to support, and so on. The equation is simple and the execution is pivotal, but living S.A.L.S.A. is exceptional.

Reflections

_____

_____

_____

_____

_____

_____

_____

_____

_____

_____

_____

_____

_____

_____

_____

_____

_____

_____

_____

Reflections

_____

_____

_____

_____

_____

_____

_____

_____

_____

_____

_____

_____

_____

_____

_____

_____

_____

_____

Reflections

_____

_____

_____

_____

_____

_____

_____

_____

_____

_____

_____

_____

_____

_____

_____

_____

_____

_____

_____

S.A.L.S.A. Moves All of Us...

I am a quiet, reserved, thoughtful, and shy person—or at least I used to be before I found this music and this dance. I have to give you some back story for the whole thing to make sense: my late husband was Cuban-American, and he introduced me to the Latin culture and its music. We tried to dance Salsa a few times—not in the way I know it now, but just to have fun and to move to the music.

A year after he passed, some friends tried to cheer me up by taking me to a Salsa club. I saw a couple there spinning and doing these dynamic moves. They seemed so con-nected and alive! I decided right there that I wanted that (and needed that), so I started classes the next week.

Dancing has helped me find a part of myself that was buried and dormant. I have had to accept my limitations but have also learned how to let them go—a balancing act of passion and shyness. Now I leap when I'm nervous or feeling silly and let myself connect to the other person and to myself. It has been a remarkable journey for me, and the longer I dance, the more I continue to grow and find this balance.

Kristin A.

I confess that I knew almost nothing about Salsa's cultural meaning, excitement, and appreciation until I met you. I was aware that the genre existed and knew of its popularity in Latin America and the Caribbean, but I was much more attracted to R&B, Hip-Hop, Pop, and other Latin genres.

Meeting you and becoming acquainted with your passion for Salsa has sprouted a personal attraction in me toward the genre. Knowing that you appreciate and acknowledge a culture opposite of yours is a great Learning experience. Not only do you satisfactorily speak Spanish, but you also do a great job of dancing Salsa with soul and enjoyment. Unlike me, you've consumed the cultural importance that Salsa rhythms convey. Salsa is more than romance and dance: it's a testimonial to encouragement and enthusiasm that also sponsors identity. Your passion for Salsa exudes this.

I know that through S.A.L.S.A. and taking part in its cultural movement, you've "Found Your Rhythm to Success" and gained personal identity. As your friend, I **S**upport, **A**ccept, and admire you for such goals and accomplishments and fully encourage you to continue **S**triving.

I can't say that Salsa has impacted me personally, but I can say that the influence that it has had on you has showered me with the same passion. I now want to lose my lack of interest and **S**trive to **A**ccept this cultural movement—to participate in the many pleasures of this testimony that contains the benefit of Exercise, Expanding Social Life, and Gaining Self-Confidence as well as Social Dancing Skills and Balancing Life!

Support. **A**ct. **L**earn. **S**trive. **A**ccept.

LET'S ALL S.A.L.S.A.!

Much Love & Support,

Yessica M.

I suppose I hadn't thought much about Salsa in the terms of S.A.L.S.A. initially. It's funny, because as I read the breakdown of the words, it came to me full circle. I am not a big time Salsa dancer, but I enjoy it when I have the chance to go out dancing or see others dancing. I also realize what the words mean as they relate to me with S.A.L.S.A. Salsa is a mixture of different things coming together, and so is the dance.

For me, your breakdown of "Support" was particularly important. When you're learning how to dance, support is a part of it—whether it's supporting yourself with foundation or helping your partner. Life is a parallel of this: you want to find great support in order to keep you going. When there is someone special in your life, a friend or otherwise, giving that support is equally as important. Through my times of struggle, relying on support is what I've been able to find the most helpful. I know that I have support in the right places from the right people. That is what we all need; whether or not you dance another day in your life, that first S says and offers so much.

Derrick C.

This program scared me. I saw the name and knew it'd be fun and might involve some kind of interaction, but the word "Action" never really occurred to me until you said, "Everyone, get up!" I thought "Ummm...no, he didn't just say that!" But then you broke it down.

What does it mean to act? What does it mean to do something? Sometimes it means to make a move when we don't know everything and to take a chance on ourselves. Completing something like S.A.L.S.A. has let me know that, piece by piece, anything can be possible. I have more faith in myself and will continue to push for myself and the people around me.

Jennifer S.

I have learned so much from dancing. Salsa is a blast of course, even if you're not sure what you're doing. It has helped me to meet different people and become more open to my surroundings. I know that if you're reading this, maybe you were just like me at some point: shy, a little insecure, and not quite sure where you fit in around campus or in life. S.A.L.S.A. is life, though, and it can help you through—whether you experience the actual dance portion or not.

You will need support, action, learning, striving, and acceptance throughout your life. The sooner you realize how much those things can help you, the better. Take a chance and, if nothing else, think about what each of the words in S.A.L.S.A. stand for and go from there.

Steven J.

S.A.L.S.A. Diary

_____

_____

_____

_____

_____

_____

_____

_____

_____

_____

_____

_____

_____

_____

_____

_____

_____

_____

_____

_____

_____

_____

S.A.L.S.A. Diary

_____

_____

_____

_____

_____

_____

_____

_____

_____

_____

_____

_____

_____

_____

_____

_____

_____

_____

_____

_____

S.A.L.S.A. Diary

S.A.L.S.A. Diary

_____

_____

_____

_____

_____

_____

_____

_____

_____

_____

_____

_____

_____

_____

_____

_____

_____

_____

_____

S.A.L.S.A. Diary

S.A.L.S.A. Diary

_____

_____

_____

_____

_____

_____

_____

_____

_____

_____

_____

_____

_____

_____

_____

_____

_____

S.A.L.S.A. Diary

S.A.L.S.A. Diary

_____

_____

_____

_____

_____

_____

_____

_____

_____

_____

_____

_____

_____

_____

_____

_____

_____

_____

_____

S.A.L.S.A. Diary

_____

_____

_____

_____

_____

_____

_____

_____

_____

_____

_____

_____

_____

_____

_____

_____

_____

_____

_____

S.A.L.S.A. Diary

_____

_____

_____

_____

_____

_____

_____

_____

_____

_____

_____

_____

_____

_____

_____

_____

_____

_____

The ABCs in Your Rhythm to Success

This section is designed to get you thinking about lots of different aspects of life. Each letter of the alphabet is included, and some letters will get more than one word, but just like mom and dad told you when you were growing up, some of these things you'll have to figure out on your own. I'm going give you some tips on how to master success through diversity, but this is only the beginning.

A – Ability. Now, if we're really talking about mastering success through diversity, ability is a huge A. The ability to be open up to anything possible in any circumstance is essential to overcoming life's obstacles.

Reflections

_____

_____

_____

_____

_____

_____

_____

_____

_____

_____

_____

_____

_____

_____

_____

_____

_____

A – Attitude. Attitude is everything in achieving success. Having the right perspective makes it clear that it's your responsibility to take full advantage of your ability in every situation, making diversity a clear focus of everything you do.

Reflections

_____

_____

_____

_____

_____

_____

_____

_____

_____

_____

_____

_____

_____

_____

_____

_____

_____

_____

_____

B – Beauty. To fully understand diversity, you have to recognize that everything that exists in the world is beautiful. No matter whether it's the little things or the big things, the kids from different backgrounds playing together or whole countries, cultures, and ways of life, beautiful things are what make the world evolve. To really master success through diversity, you have to understand that anything you can touch, smell, see, taste, or experience is a beautiful thing. They might come in different shapes and sizes, but they all share that common link.

Reflections

_____

_____

_____

_____

_____

_____

_____

_____

_____

_____

_____

_____

_____

_____

_____

_____

_____

_____

_____

C – Confidence. To be successful, you have to be confident in who you are, where you are, what you believe, what you say, and what you do every single moment of every single day. What's more, you have to do these things while appreciating and respecting that difference of opinion is the key diversity that strengthens us. We all have to be confident enough to believe that it's okay to accept other views and to understand them.

Reflections

_____

_____

_____

_____

_____

_____

_____

_____

_____

_____

_____

_____

_____

_____

_____

_____

_____

_____

C – Care. Care for the people around you, because we all need the support of others as we move on in life. Stay mindful of other **cultures**, as well—and of the **commitment** that we all have to look after one another in whatever ways we can.

Reflections

_____

_____

_____

_____

_____

_____

_____

_____

_____

_____

_____

_____

_____

_____

_____

_____

_____

_____

D – Dedication/Desire. To do anything and every-thing, even when people tell you something can't be done, you need to desire success and be dedicated to what will come ahead. The more we all do these things, the better off we all will be.

Reflections

_____

_____

_____

_____

_____

_____

_____

_____

_____

_____

_____

_____

_____

_____

_____

_____

_____

_____

E – Education. From our first day at school on-ward, education is critical to our lives. It's not li-mited to the classroom, either: if we never find out about what goes on in the wider world, all of our teachers' efforts will have been wasted. No matter how many books you read, if you can't apply them to the outside world and to the people you affect, you may as well not have picked them up in the first place. When properly used, education is a core mo-tivation to our continuous evolution, helping to bat-tle and conquer all of society's various types of per-secutions.

Reflections

_____

_____

_____

_____

_____

_____

_____

_____

_____

_____

_____

_____

_____

_____

_____

_____

_____

_____

F – Fulfillment (of our minds, bodies, and souls).
The greatest fears are those that are related to failure. Without failure, though, there can't be any success. Without good, there can't be any bad. Appreciating success is so much more powerful when you look back at where you could have been—so don't be afraid. Failure is just the next step to success, so be free to embrace it! Failure creates!

Reflections

_____

_____

_____

_____

_____

_____

_____

_____

_____

_____

_____

_____

_____

_____

_____

_____

_____

_____

G – God. This one's about mastering success through diversity by recognizing that there's someone higher than yourself. No matter what higher being you believe in, always stay thankful for everything given to you: it's all part of the path we travel.

Reflections

_____

_____

_____

_____

_____

_____

_____

_____

_____

_____

_____

_____

_____

_____

_____

_____

_____

_____

G – Greatness. World-renowned speaker Les Brown often says: "Manifest your greatness, because sometimes good just isn't good enough." Greatness is exactly that! Always strive to be your best.

Reflections

_____

_____

_____

_____

_____

_____

_____

_____

_____

_____

_____

_____

_____

_____

_____

_____

_____

_____

H – Humility. Awwwwwwww, yeah. Can you believe I put that in this book? In all cultures, ways of life, and experiences, we have to be able to accept others and their mistakes and our own. We don't always have to be right. If you're truly looking to master success through diversity, choose to be humble: it can go a long way, especially if it aids someone around you.

Reflections

_____

_____

_____

_____

_____

_____

_____

_____

_____

_____

_____

_____

_____

_____

_____

_____

_____

_____

H – Handicapped. This is a powerful word, and if we don't shift our immediate responses to it, we can end up focusing on the wrong things and drawing senseless conclusions. I've actually heard people say that handicapped people put a strain on society, for example. Are you kidding me? I see plenty of able-bodied individuals who are strains on society—and the correct term for those with disabilities is "special needs," anyway. If you really shift your reaction to what being handicapped means, you begin to realize that diversity is everything. Sometimes those who are less capable physically or mentally have more heart and dedication than those who have everything! Is that real enough for you? It's amazing how society continues to place stigmas on people who work twice as hard as average able-bodied people to live and survive. When you think about this, who's really handicapped??? If we handicap ourselves with what we think, we become our own worst enemies within cultures, beliefs, and right in our homes. We are all beautiful people doing beautiful things. Dedicating ourselves to looking at people as individuals and equals will, God-willing, have an everlasting effect on this world of diversity.

Reflections

_____

_____

_____

_____

_____

_____

_____

_____

_____

_____

_____

_____

_____

_____

_____

_____

_____

_____

I – "I" can do this. Everything in life starts with "I" because if you want to master success through diversity, you have to know that change is up to you. You have to get up every morning, look in the mirror, and say to yourself, "I can do better, and I will do better. I can do anything I want to with the help of the people around me, because that will strengthen us all." It's also helpful to say, "I will educate the world about the importance of integrity and help to decrease the insincerity and ignorance that I see around me." This last point is something we should all do from time to time, as it's vital to spread the message of diversity—our gateway to success today, tomorrow, and in the future.

Reflections

_____

_____

_____

_____

_____

_____

_____

_____

_____

_____

_____

_____

_____

_____

_____

_____

_____

_____

J – Journey. Embracing diversity is a major part in the journey of life, as anyone who is successful in anything will tell you. The people we meet and experience as we go forward humble those of us who keep our minds open, because they help us to remember that we always have something left to learn. Even the longest of journeys begins with a single step too, so never be afraid to start accepting the world around you.

Reflections

_____

_____

_____

_____

_____

_____

_____

_____

_____

_____

_____

_____

_____

_____

_____

_____

_____

_____

K – Knowledge. "If you think knowledge is power, you're not completely right. What you do with knowledge is power." Does that make sense? There are plenty of intelligent people in the world who don't share their gifts or put their knowledge into action. We were not made to be human libraries. Instead, we are all messengers who have the ability to induce change and lead powerfully, putting what we know to good effect. Knowledge is empowering, and action alongside it is unparalleled. Don't waste your knowledge on idle thoughts because when you do this, you're also wasting precious time. We don't have long to make a difference in our lives, so every second counts.

Reflections

_____

_____

_____

_____

_____

_____

_____

_____

_____

_____

_____

_____

_____

_____

_____

_____

_____

L – Limitations. You are the only person who can put limits on yourself. As you continue to grow, you will discover that successful people are just individuals who don't allow others to limit their possibilities, and they definitely don't limit themselves, either. The only limits that should exist in your life are speed limits on the road. We have what it takes to be limitless, so we have to recognize our power. Laugh a few times every day as well! You'll be amazed at what it can do.

Reflections

_____

_____

_____

_____

_____

_____

_____

_____

_____

_____

_____

_____

_____

_____

_____

_____

_____

_____

M – Motivation. Continue to seek out ways to motivate yourself and the people around you. That word itself should move you!

Reflections

_____

_____

_____

_____

_____

_____

_____

_____

_____

_____

_____

_____

_____

_____

_____

_____

_____

_____

N – Next. When I travel to different places to speak, I ask people what their favorite four-letter word is. I hear all kinds of things for answers, often including "love," "luck," "home," "pray," and "cash" (and a few of those other more colorful words that people use from time to time as well!). My favorite word is "next." It's an important word because it lets you know that there's always something else waiting for you in the future. Being a leader and mastering success through diversity doesn't mean immediately getting everything you want whenever you try for it. We have to understand that things can change, so not every answer will always be yes. If someone says, "Maybe later," for example, just move on and say _____. There'll be another opportunity waiting for you at another place or at another time. If someone says, "I'll think about it," you say _____. If someone says, "You can't possibly succeed doing that," you say _____. Keep on practicing this: we're all just a product of our most dominant thoughts. Keep that in mind! NEXT.

Reflections

O – Opportunity. If you kick down every door you come to, you'll never have to wait for an answer to a knock again. I believe in kicking every door down, as it makes sure that you take advantage of every opportunity you're ever given. As we meet people, especially those from different states, countries, or walks of life, we only do ourselves and others justice by making the most of those opportunities. The most successful people in the world even treat adversities and obstacles as opportunities, as overcoming them takes you one step closer to your goal.

****

Let's stop here for a moment. If you embrace everything that these words mean, you'll start to get a different perspective on the world. Take the four-letter word "luck" mentioned above, for example: you'll soon be able to twist its meaning. Instead of thinking that "luck is for those who are ill-prepared," you'll start to think that "luck is where opportunity and preparedness meet."

Whoa! This is good stuff! I hope you're making a few notes or highlighting. Which words discussed so far have particularly applied to you? As you continue to engage with this book and its ideas, which words will you focus on?

Without further hesitation, let's continue.

Reflections

_____

_____

_____

_____

_____

_____

_____

_____

_____

_____

_____

_____

_____

_____

_____

_____

_____

_____

_____

P – Preparedness. Staying prepared is essential to meeting your goals. There's even a phrase to help you remember this: proper prior planning prevents poor performance. Say that every day as a reminder to yourself that greatness is within your reach so long as you're willing to prepare for it. Once you've done this, it's also important to persevere in your actions as well. You might come across difficulties, but everything can be overcome if you believe in your strength.

Reflections

_____

_____

_____

_____

_____

_____

_____

_____

_____

_____

_____

_____

_____

_____

_____

_____

_____

_____

Q – Questions. If you're going to be successful and lead, you have to ask questions. You have to be willing to rectify your own ignorance and not settle into the blissfulness of the unknown. We're often scared of the things we don't know, but this fear can be remedied if we question it. This applies to even the biggest areas of life; great leaders such as Martin Luther King Jr., Rosa Parks, and John F. Kennedy may have made great progress, but we can only continue to move forward if we never stop querying the things around us.

Reflections

_____

_____

_____

_____

_____

_____

_____

_____

_____

_____

_____

_____

_____

_____

_____

_____

_____

R – Racism. That's right—did you really think I'd let this book end without mentioning the R-word? It has to be included so that student leaders of institutions throughout the country and the world can realize that it still exists. Racists don't always say the N-word and other derogatory remarks, but they're still be among us. Always remaining mindful is the key to protecting ourselves and others from hate. Battle racism with excellence and acceptance; leading by example will continually aid our growth.

Reflections

_____

_____

_____

_____

_____

_____

_____

_____

_____

_____

_____

_____

_____

_____

_____

_____

_____

_____

_____

R – R.E.A.D.Y. As I heard Karl V. Bell of Boston College say in 1999, you have to be "Really Excited About Dedicating Yourself." Every one of us has to be R.E.A.D.Y., because if you aren't excited about what you're doing, then why should I be? As a leader, being R.E.A.D.Y. will also help you to outdo your competition at every turn.

Reflections

_____

_____

_____

_____

_____

_____

_____

_____

_____

_____

_____

_____

_____

_____

_____

_____

_____

_____

_____

_____

S – Surrounding (yourself). Two people have inspired me more than anyone else: they're my parents, Stan and Patricia Pearson. You may be wondering what they have to do with you, but I'll get to that. They've lived their lives as examples of how to overcome racism, struggle, and poverty. In doing this, they've made everything possible for their children and everyone they've come into contact with. We all have to surround ourselves with people like this—people who live as positive examples. Not everyone is raised by their parents, of course, but we all have individuals in our lives who can make us better people in some way, shape, or form. SURROUND YOURSELF WITH THOSE PEOPLE!

Reflections

_____

_____

_____

_____

_____

_____

_____

_____

_____

_____

_____

_____

_____

_____

_____

_____

_____

_____

S – Sacrifice. It's easy to forget that the road has already been paved for us in some way, shape, or form, and many people—both young adults and more mature ones—regularly do so. Somewhere along the line, people have given up their freedom in some way so that we can give ourselves over to our dreams and goals. Diversity is about having a real understanding and appreciation for the people who came before us and also for the road that we are paving for the people who will come after.

Reflections

_____

_____

_____

_____

_____

_____

_____

_____

_____

_____

_____

_____

_____

_____

_____

_____

_____

_____

T – Teaching. One of the best tools that we all are born with is the ability to teach. For those who can't teach with their mouths, they can teach with their eyes. For those who can't see, they can teach through song; diversity is about knowing that a song is nothing but words with rhythm attached to them, so of course we can teach through song. A key lesson in teaching is never to underestimate the power of a working mind in any way. We are all students of the world, so let us teach one another as we go forth.

Reflections

_____

_____

_____

_____

_____

_____

_____

_____

_____

_____

_____

_____

_____

_____

_____

_____

_____

T – Time. Time is usually taken for granted. As we continue to grow, we should do our best to use time and not to let time use us. There won't always be tomorrow, so thank God for the day you've been given and pray for an even better day to come to-morrow. Do you best to use your time with balance as well: it should include family, friends, love, plen-ty of laughter, and doing at least one thing that you enjoy doing as often as possible. Find that activity that frees you from the world and that makes you smile, and then do it. Diversity is about making the most of the time that we have.

Reflections

_____

_____

_____

_____

_____

_____

_____

_____

_____

_____

_____

_____

_____

_____

_____

_____

_____

_____

T – Truth. Truth is mandatory in everything. Not only is it imperative that we are true to others, but we should also be true to ourselves. If you are reading this, know that if you only ever rely on the truth, you will always be able to walk with your head help up high in pride.

Reflections

_____

_____

_____

_____

_____

_____

_____

_____

_____

_____

_____

_____

_____

_____

_____

_____

_____

_____

U – **Understanding.** Being able to understand things is necessary because not every situation you get involved in will always be the greatest situation. No matter what it is, though, there are pieces of it that you can learn from if you take the time to understand what really happened. Also take the time to understand people: we can all be so different at times, but those differences can bring us closer together. The more we understand that, the better.

Reflections

_____

_____

_____

_____

_____

_____

_____

_____

_____

_____

_____

_____

_____

_____

_____

_____

_____

_____

V – Victory. This is what you need to find in everything that happens to you. We've all heard about finding the good in bad situations, and that good really does always exist. You might just sometimes have to work to find it.

Reflections

_____

_____

_____

_____

_____

_____

_____

_____

_____

_____

_____

_____

_____

_____

_____

_____

_____

W – When. People often ask me when it'll be the right time to get things moving/take care of business/make an important decision. I always tell them the same thing: right now. There's no time like the present, so take the time to make the time. It's up to you to make your "when" happen now.

Reflections

_____

_____

_____

_____

_____

_____

_____

_____

_____

_____

_____

_____

_____

_____

_____

_____

_____

_____

X – X-ray. This word might seem like an easy choice for this letter, huh? You might be shaking your head, but this will make sense. When you get an X-ray done, you're looking at the inside of something—often to see whether something's broken so you can fix it. Try to take this one step further and use your own "personal X-rays" for self-improvement: look inside yourself to see what needs to be taken care of.

Reflections

_____

_____

_____

_____

_____

_____

_____

_____

_____

_____

_____

_____

_____

_____

_____

_____

_____

Y – **Yesterday.** Yesterday is gone. Whatever you completed or didn't complete is final, because the day has passed and you can never get it back. You can look at yesterday for guidance and reference, of course, but you can't dwell on it. If you do this, your todays won't ever move forward. Do you want tomorrow to be another failure??? Our time to live is NOW.

Reflections

_____

_____

_____

_____

_____

_____

_____

_____

_____

_____

_____

_____

_____

_____

_____

_____

_____

_____

Z – Zest. We need to have a zest for life. Sometimes people ask me why I smile so much or why I'm so happy. I have things going on in my life, and sometimes they can be tough to deal with, but life is here, so I do my best to enjoy it and have that zest for it. I follow the steps that I've written to the best of my ability so that I'm doing more than talking and writing about things. I'm being them.

Our Twists and Turns

Life and dancing have many parallels in what they mean and what they make us experience. When you dance, for example, you might experience lots of twists and turns or be led around by someone else. Life will give you just the same things. They won't all be fun or earth-shatteringly important, but every event will help you to get closer to your goals. We are here, and we are made to Support, Act, Learn, Strive, and Accept.

I hope this book has provided some insight and inspiration for you to take on your journey. It's only one piece of your puzzle, however. Only you are capable of finding the rest and putting it together.

68058347R00078

Made in the USA
Charleston, SC
04 March 2017